"To all who come to this happy place, welcome. Disneyland is your land. Here age relives fond memories of the past . . . and here youth may savor the challenge and promise of the future. Disneyland is dedicated to the ideals, dreams, and the hard facts that have created America . . . with the hope that it will be a source of joy and inspiration in the world."

—Walt Disney

Disneyland Park

Disneyland Park creates a thousand different memories, from joyful times in a kingdom of storybook enchantment to a thrilling journey into the realm of pioneers in the Old West. The exotic regions of Asia, Africa, India, and the South Pacific offer exploration and adventure, and there's always a place to relax in a down-home country setting. Discovery and fun abound at a launching pad for space-age attractions into imagination and beyond, and a three-dimensional cartoon hometown for Mickey Mouse and his friends. It is truly "the happiest place on earth."

Main Street, U.S.A.®

Main Street, U.S.A., is the essence of hometown America at the dawn of the twentieth century. The scent of freshly baked cakes and candies, the steady clip-clop of the horse-drawn streetcar, and the twinkling pin lights outlining the gingerbread trim of the buildings evoke a small-town atmosphere. "I love the nostalgic myself," Walt said. "I hope we never lose some things of the past."

Bells and whistles herald the arrival of the Disneyland Railroad's four steam trains. Rows of specialty shops carry a colorful variety of old-time merchandise. At night, the thoroughfare glows in the flickering light of gaslit streetlamps. Main Street, U.S.A., is engaging proof that the best of yesterday can still be found today.

Adventureland®

Exotic colors catch the eye among the lush landscape. Rustic colonial architecture stands between bazaars straight out of the pages of an *Arabian Nights* adventure. Don your pith helmet and enter the land where the beat of native drums echo around you.

"Many of us dream of traveling to mysterious far-off regions of the world," said Walt. "To create a land that would make this dream a reality we pictured ourselves far from civilization, in the remote jungles of Africa and Asia. Here is adventure. Here is romance. Here is mystery. Tropical rivers silently flow into the unknown. The unbelievable splendor of exotic flowers . . . the eerie sounds of the jungle . . . with eyes that are always watching. This is Adventureland—the wonderland of nature's own design."

Lost Delta, India, circa 1935.
Artifacts lead to a jungle base camp where the renowned archaeologist Indiana Jones™ has made his latest archaeological discovery: The Temple of the Forbidden Eye. The temple is a lasting tribute to the natives' patron deity, Mara. Can Indy help his fellow explorers escape the dreadful price they must pay should they look into the eyes of the angry goddess?

Amidst a canopy of giant bamboo, ficus, palm, and coral trees course the jungle rivers of the world—Nile, Zambezi, Congo, Mekong, Irrawaddy, Ganges. Here are seen the trappings of primitive civilizations and vanished cultures: spears, shields, ceremonial masks, and raiment native to tribal life along the equator. But jungle life is never boring, as elephants frolic in a pool, squirting water at bold travelers, and a rhino helps a lost safari get the point of adventure and travel.

A towering treetop home in the vastness of Africa provides shelter for Tarzan, Jane, and their animal friends. Musical pots and pans provide a symphonic sound track while scientific experiments abound, including the "Tarzan Yella-phone."

José, Michael, Fritz, and Pierre are the hosts of The Enchanted Tiki Room, set in the splendor of Polynesia, where "the birds sing words and the flowers croon." A sudden tropical storm with thunder and lightning does nothing to dampen spirits "In the Tiki, Tiki, Tiki, Tiki, Tiki Room."

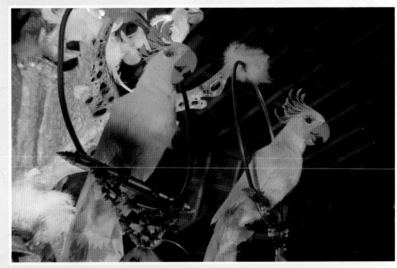

Frontierland®

As Walt held, "All of us have cause to be proud of our country's history, shaped by the pioneering spirit of our forefathers. Here we experience the story of our country's past—the colorful drama of Frontier America in the exciting days of the covered wagon and the stage-coach to the advent of the railroad and the romantic riverboat. It is to these hardy pioneers, men of vision, faith, and courage, that we dedicate Frontierland."

From the windswept peaks of Big Thunder Mountain to the shores of the Rivers of America to the raucous and dusty desert southwest, Frontierland is an amalgam of sights and sounds that authentically conjure up images from America's western expansion. Come by land, water, or rail—pioneer days live on in Frontierland.

Set amid the rustic beauty of an authentic-looking gold-mining town, Big Thunder Mountain Railroad is "the wildest ride in the wilderness" you've ever hollered, rooted, and hooted through! Runaway mine trains race around towering buttes, dive into dangerous gulches, and plunge deep into foreboding chilly caverns filled with bats and phosphorescent pools. Intrepid passengers careen past raging waterfalls, coyotes, rattlesnakes, and twirling opossums before finally encountering a deafening earthquake from which the mountain gets its name.

The *Mark Twain,* a stately steam-powered stern-wheeler, gently paddles the waters around the secret hideaways on Tom Sawyer Island, as the Sailing Ship *Columbia* presents an impressive sight re-creating the first American windjammer to circle the globe. The diverse watercraft plying the man-made Rivers of America serve as reminders that keelboat men, captains, and pilots rank alongside cowboys and sodbusters as Western pioneers.

At nighttime, the Rivers of America host "Fantasmic!," a thrilling spectacular set in a fantasy of Mickey Mouse's vivid imagination and a pioneer in its own right of multimedia entertainment, including lasers, black lights, fireworks, fire, and animated images on huge mist screens. Laughs Mickey, "Some imagination, huh?!"

Critter Country®

Nestled in a lazy corner of the back-woods is Critter Country, a world where the alligators, rabbits, bears, opossums, foxes, owls, and frogs are as neighborly as they can be. It celebrates a time when the critters were closer to the folks and the folks were closer to the critters, and you might even say things were better all around. This little area of shady trees and cool streams is the perfect setting for savoring long lazy afternoons and an opportunity to simply delight in the down-home country atmosphere.

In Critter Country, it's always one of those zip-a-dee-doo-dah days—the kind of day where you can't open your mouth without a song jumpin' right out.

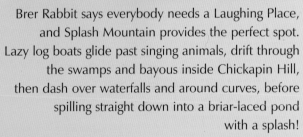

Brer Rabbit says everybody needs a Laughing Place, and Splash Mountain provides the perfect spot. Lazy log boats glide past singing animals, drift through the swamps and bayous inside Chickapin Hill, then dash over waterfalls and around curves, before spilling straight down into a briar-laced pond with a splash!

New Orleans Square®

Pastel-colored buildings embellished with wrought-iron tracery face onto streets as picturesque as in the French Quarter of two centuries ago. Sidewalk artists work in cloistered arcades, and musicians gather daily for a session of hand-clappin', thigh-tappin' Dixieland jazz. New Orleans Square casts a spell rich with tales of swashbuckling pirates and ghouls, ghosts, and goblins.

Within its sheltered courtyards and winding streets, Southern grace and charm abound. The aromas of chicory and freshly baked fritters fill the air, while the billowing white sails of a mighty galleon can be seen in the distance. From blossoming magnolia trees to authentic gas lamps, New Orleans Square evokes the elegance of a land filled with magic, mystery, and a sense of discovery.

Welcome foolish mortals,
to The Haunted Mansion—
home to 999 ghosts, but
there's always room for
one more! There's no
shortage of hot and cold
running chills in this stately
antebellum mansion—and
each room is furnished
with wall-to-wall creaks.
All the spirits are dying to
meet you as you tour the
house in your own private
Doom Buggy.

"Ye come seeking adventure and salty old pirates, aye. Sure you come to the proper place, but keep a weather eye open! . . . There be thundering pirates lurking in every cove."

Misty moonlit bayous . . . cascading waterfalls . . . grinning skeletons . . . a harbor port under siege . . . "It be too late to alter course, matey." Voyage past pirate plunder, dodge cannonballs, and escape from a town set ablaze by salty dogs. The merry buccaneers here are always ready to steal a laugh.

Fantasyland®

Within the magical Old World setting of Fantasyland, guests can fly through the London night to Never Land, see an elephant fly, take a spin in a giant teacup, and brave the icy thrills of the Matterhorn Bobsleds. Sleeping Beauty Castle beckons you to Fantasyland— where every corner holds a bit of the magic of dreams come true. If Disneyland has a heart, it is surely here.

"Here is the world of imagination, hopes, and dreams," said Walt. "In this timeless land of enchantment, the age of chivalry, magic, and make-believe are reborn, and fairy tales come true. Fantasyland is dedicated to the young and the young-in-heart."

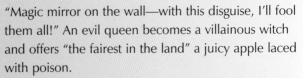

"Magic mirror on the wall—with this disguise, I'll fool them all!" An evil queen becomes a villainous witch and offers "the fairest in the land" a juicy apple laced with poison.

"Come on everybody—here we go!" Peter Pan fights his nemesis Captain Hook before sailing on a pixie-dusted galleon into starry skies, while Pinocchio and his faithful conscience Jiminy Cricket try to avoid fateful encounters.

Don't be late as the White Rabbit leads Alice into Wonderland to a very merry Unbirthday Party, a fantastical garden of flowers, and a narrow escape from the March of Cards.

In a different English countryside, J. Thaddeus Toad drives his all-new motorcar and takes off on a ride that sends him merrily through several wild adventures.

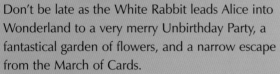

Timothy Q. Mouse stands in command at the center of Dumbo the Flying Elephant. Water sprays from a fountain, and cogs, gears, and pulleys help the world's most famous flying pachyderm, "the eighth wonder of the world," soar high.

Brightly painted cups and saucers whirl, twirl, swirl, and spin and spin and spin in a life-sized Unbirthday Party under colorful Chinese paper lanterns and clusters of large trumpet-shaped white flowers.

Nerves tingle on a breathtaking bobsled run down the snowy slopes of Matterhorn Mountain. Pass giant icicles and ice crystals, twist and turn through windswept tunnels and clouds of fog, and encounter the terrifying Abominable Snowman before splashing to a stop in an alpine lake.

Drift along on the "Happiest Cruise That Ever Sailed," saluting the children of the world, who speak the international language of goodwill. Help the Casey Jr. Circus Train chug and puff his way through the hills and valleys of Storybook Land, cheerfully proclaiming "I think I can, I think I can," or ride astride a prancing steed from the Knights of the Round Table on one of the largest carousels in the world.

Mickey's Toontown®

Legend has it that Mickey Mouse founded the three-acre community called Toontown in the 1930s as a retreat from the bustle of Hollywood. Until its opening in 1993, Toontown was kept secret, the only human allowed inside being Walt Disney. Fortunately, as Disneyland Park grew, Mickey decided to open Toontown to the public.

Bursting with color and frenetic energy, you'll find the population's just a bit "goofy" here, where the Clockenspiel announces the arrival of Toon residents with bells, whistles, and horns and even produces a bouquet of flowers. The official seal of Toontown contains, well, a seal. When heading for a visit to this hometown, be sure to pack your funny bone.

The Jolly Trolley provides a rambling two-way trip through Mickey's Toontown, traveling past the Gag Factory, Max's Hair Restoration, and the 3rd Little Piggy Bank with a decidedly "loco" motion. At Mickey's House, the welcome mat is always out for a friendly four-fingered handshake, and Minnie offers visitors a sweet time, including the recipe for her Famous Chewy Cheesy Chip cookies.

The Toontown Tourism Board can offer a fun-filled time, whether it's exploring the treetop home of Chip 'n' Dale or aboard Donald's Boat, the *Miss Daisy*. Take control of the wheel in Roger Rabbit's Car Toon Spin, or enjoy Goofy's Bounce House, which will have you literally bouncing off the walls. In addition to being entertaining, this colorful community prides itself on being environmentally conscious—there's even a recycling bin for used gloves.

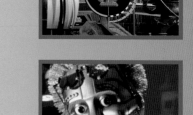

Tomorrowland®

Walt described Tomorrowland as "A vista into a world of wondrous ideas, signifying man's achievements . . . a step into the future, with predictions of constructive things to come. Tomorrow offers new frontiers in science, adventure, and ideals: the challenge of outer space and the hope for a peaceful and unified world."

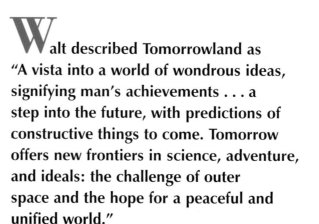

No matter how far away guests are transported or how far into the future they travel, Tomorrowland itself will always remain timeless, just as dreams are timeless. With its whirling spaceships, zooming rocket vehicles, lush vegetation, and kinetic sculptures and fountains, Tomorrowland builds upon Walt's original vision and presents an exciting look beyond the stars to a future full of promise and hope.

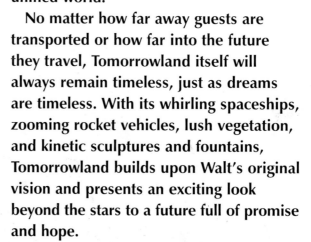

Tomorrowland adventures evolve from both science fact and science fiction in this land of the imagination and beyond. See the world from a different perspective while sailing in radiant cosmos-colored rocket ships or shrinking down to "mouse size." Pilot a Space Cruiser and fire personal laser cannons to protect the peace of outer space from the forces of Emperor Zurg. Exciting, futuristic, and cutting-edge, Tomorrowland is well worthy of living up to its billing as "A World on the Move."

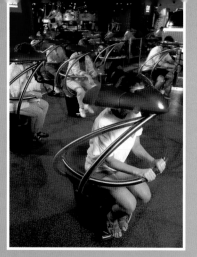

Space Mountain passengers can now enjoy a re-Imagineered ride for the twenty-first century as they roar through the darkness of deep space and race past giant meteors and shooting stars. An all-new, edgy sound track accompanies this first-hand look into space, which ends with a finale of spectacular lighting effects. In Innoventions, two levels of interactive "edutainment" offer a hands-on look at how creative technical developments will improve our lives for the future.

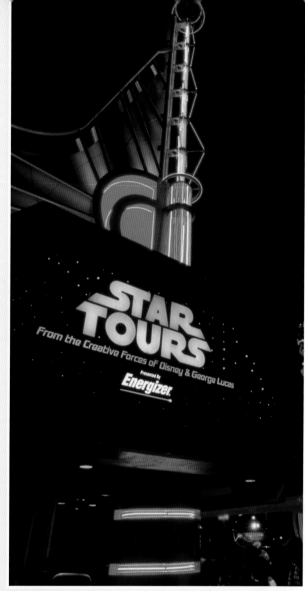

Tomorrowland has always been a proving ground for transportation systems of the future. On its "Highway in the Sky," the Disneyland Monorail has carried millions of passengers in comfortable, sleek, stream-lined cars. On the Starspeeder 2000, passengers enjoy a decidedly wilder trip through an asteroid field, narrowly escaping an intergalactic dogfight and successfully maneuvering through the dangerous chasms of a Death Star.

The grandeur, lore, and energy of California find an exciting showcase in Disney's California Adventure Park. The Golden State's majestic landscapes, rich cultural history, and electric lifestyle are celebrated in fun-filled attractions and wondrous adventures that travel through places in the past, the present, the future . . . and those only found in the imagination. Explore high desert airfields, experience a most unordinary elevator ride to the edge of reality, see things from a "bug's-eye" perspective, or swing around the inside of a huge California orange in a park that is as diverse and full of surprises as the land that inspired it.

Golden State®

The Golden State area, with its variety of rustic landscapes, distinctive cuisines, and exciting rides, exemplifies California's rich diversity of land and people. Under the watchful eye of Grizzly Peak, thrill seekers can race down swirling white water on an exhilarating raft ride, fly over the beauty of dense redwood forests and snowcapped mountains, or get a taste of the hearty ethnic foods enjoyed along the state's rocky coastline.

The area is divided into a variety of regions, all different in topography, culture, and history. From the northern Sierra to the deserts, the ocean, the valleys, and vineyards, the rich heritage and natural beauty is celebrated in a land where opportunity is truly "golden."

Fly high above the breathtaking natural beauty of the state in Soarin' Over California as it takes wing over the awesome beauty of Yosemite, glides over a Tahoe ski slope, and races above the desert floor, accompanied by six Air Force Thunderbirds. Then it's time for some "serious rafting" on the Grizzly River Run, where the motto is "The Wetter, the Better." This proves true when the white-knuckle flume ride careens over a waterfall into a wild-water rampage and ends with a soaking plunge into an erupting geyser field.

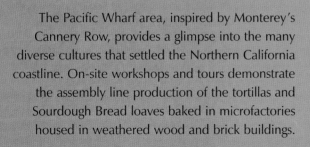

The Pacific Wharf area, inspired by Monterey's Cannery Row, provides a glimpse into the many diverse cultures that settled the Northern California coastline. On-site workshops and tours demonstrate the assembly line production of the tortillas and Sourdough Bread loaves baked in microfactories housed in weathered wood and brick buildings.

a bug's land®

Look at life from a bug's-eye view in this imaginative land inspired by the Disney/Pixar film *A Bug's Life*, featuring Flik and his insect friends. Whether it's riding in "hot-air balloons" fashioned from leaves and take-out boxes on Flik's Flyers, tasting adventure on the back of a hungry caterpillar on Heimlich's Chew Chew Train, puddle-jumping in an over-sized garden landscape, or being driven buggy by two acrobatic gibberish-speaking pill bugs, a bug's land proves that being small is big fun.

It's Tough to be a Bug!, appropriately housed in the dark underground cave next to Bountiful Valley Farm, is a creepy, crawly 3-D movie that features Flik, Hopper, and zillions of other wriggling friends including tarantulas, termites, and the most odiferous member of the bug world, the "silent but deadly" stinkbug.

Hollywood Pictures
Backlot

Step through ornate gates onto a palm-lined boulevard of dreams and go "on location" to enjoy the glitzy world of celebrity on the Hollywood Pictures Backlot. Fun and fantasy prevail along the glittering streets, lined with Art Deco and Spanish-style facades.

Behind the scenes are hands-on demonstrations of the animator's craft, 3-D movie merriment, and a thrilling, chilling supernatural adventure based on a classic television series. Enjoy a Broadway-style show in a 2,000-seat showplace that recalls the stylish movie palaces of Hollywood's golden age or join a celebratory free-for-all dance party with irresistible music. Everyone holds a backstage pass to the glamour of movie-making in a land where there are always plenty of lights, cameras, and exciting action.

If you're looking for fun and excitement, the shows at Hollywood Pictures Backlot are just the ticket, including an ornate song-and-dance showplace, an interactive look inside the artistry of animation, and the inspired lunacy of the Muppets as their attempt to explain 3-D filmmaking to spectators goes terribly wacky.

DIRECTORY

STARDUST ROOM	MEZZANINE
HIGH SOCIETY SUITE	PENTHOUSE
BILLIARDS	LOBBY LEVEL
LIBRARY	LOBBY LEVEL
LOUNGE	LOBBY LEVEL
SUNSET ROOM	LOWER LEVEL
BEVERLY ROOM	LOWER LEVEL
FOUNTAIN ROOM	LOWER LEVEL
STEAM BATH	LOWER LEVEL
GIFT SHOP	LOWER LEVEL
TIP TOP CLUB	TOP OF THE TOWER

ANAHEIM, CALIFORNIA, MAY 5, 2004.
A new dimension in spine-tingling thrills has opened on the Hollywood Pictures Backlot.

The Hollywood Tower Hotel first opened its doors in 1928, the same year as the film debut of a certain animated mouse. This elegant and imposing structure, styled in an eclectic Pueblo Deco manner, was at the height of its popularity in the booming Hollywood community when an enigmatic occurrence forced it to close on October 31, 1939.

It was in the now-exposed elevator shafts that the mystery took place one stormy, rain-drenched evening. As one elevator ascended, lightning struck the tower, causing the lift to plunge, carrying five unlucky souls to certain doom. But before it reached the bottom of the shaft, the elevator and its passengers simply vanished, along with a large section of the hotel. Boarded up that evening, the hotel immediately emptied—staff and guests utterly unable to contend with the baffling incident. No one ever came back. The hotel remained as it was, untouched and undisturbed. Until now.

Since that fateful night, though the grounds are weed choked, the walkways cracked, and the fountains dry, the hotel seems largely unchanged within. Unread mail waits at the front desk. A forgotten set of luggage waits nearby. Visitors are now allowed to visit the crumbly yet stately landmark, where they learn to say good-bye to the real world—for they have just entered **The Twilight Zone**®.

Paradise Pier®

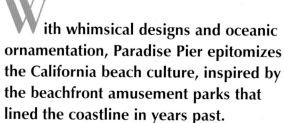

With whimsical designs and oceanic ornamentation, Paradise Pier epitomizes the California beach culture, inspired by the beachfront amusement parks that lined the coastline in years past.

Speed along a roller coaster and get a between-the-ears view of the park while circling a 360-degree loop around a silhouette of Mickey Mouse's head. Shoot up a towering rendition of a strength-testing game or ride a beautifully sculpted dolphin on an aquatic-themed carousel. Try your luck at the festive midway booths that line the boardwalk by pitching, fishing, or dunking your way to a prize, as the scent of cotton candy swirls in the air. A monument to sun, surf, and sand, Paradise Pier crackles with seaside sizzle.

PARADISE PIER

Fun in the Sun for Everyone!